✧ Easy Make & Use ✧
Mini-Reference Books
for Every Kid in Your Class

By Lisa Blau

Illustrated by Ty Pollard

SCHOLASTIC
PROFESSIONAL BOOKS

New York ✴ Toronto ✴ London ✴ Auckland ✴ Sydney
Mexico City ✴ New Delhi ✴ Hong Kong

Contents

Dear Teachers,

Congratulations on selecting **Easy Make & Use Mini-Reference Books for Every Kid in Your Class** to share with your students.

As teachers of writing, it's our responsibility to give students the "tools of the trade" and a desire to use these tools well. Each of the five mini-books in this book was designed to be user-friendly and address a specific aspect of the writing process. Students who need help with spelling and word choice can use *My Super Spelling Dictionary* and *My Marvelous Pocket Thesaurus*, while students who need to brush up on the conventions of writing can refer to *My Book of Great Grammar Rules, My Rhyming Dictionary,* and *My Wonderful Writing-Prompt Journal.*

The mini-books' easy-to-use format makes them a welcome addition to your writing program. Tuck them into your students' desks or the pockets of their writing folders for quick and easy access. A second set of mini-books can be reproduced and sent home to help kids with their homework assignments.

The mini-books are a snap to assemble. Simply copy, fold, and staple them together (as described on page 6). We've even included tips on how to introduce each mini-book, plus ready-to-go usage mini-lessons.

With this collection of mini-reference books, your students will have the tools they need to feel empowered, build literacy, and grow as independent learners.

Happy Writing!

Getting Started with the Mini-Reference Books

Assembling the Books

1. Copy the pages for each mini-book on standard 8½" x 11" paper. Make the pages *single* sided.

2. Fold the front cover/back cover in half along the dotted line, keeping the fold on the *left* side.

3. Fold the inner pages in half, keeping the fold to the *right* side.

4. Place the inner pages inside the cover in order and staple three times along the spine.

Helpful Hints:

- Place tape over the staple ends so kids don't get scratched on them.

- It's best to assemble the books before giving them to the students. A few parent volunteers can assemble an entire set of mini-books for your students in a very short time.

My Super Spelling Dictionary

Introducing the Mini-Book

Give each student an assembled mini-book. Ask students to look at the first three pages and to read the words that appear on each page. Explain that the words on each page are often spelled incorrectly. Point out the extra blank lines on each page. Tell students that new words can be added to these lines. (Tip: A good time to add new words is whenever a new spelling list is introduced to the students.)

Encourage students to refer to their *Super Spelling Dictionary* whenever they are uncertain about how a word is spelled.

Lesson Plan Idea

Make an overlay of a writing sample in which several high-frequency words have been spelled incorrectly.

Set an expectation for students by asking them to edit this particular piece of writing for its spelling. Circle the words in question with a highlighter pen. Allow time for students to look up the words in their *Super Spelling Dictionary*.

Using a new overlay, ask students to help you rewrite the story by spelling all of the incorrect words properly.

My Marvelous Thesaurus

Introducing the Mini-Book

After giving each student an assembled mini-book, take some time to identify the features of the book, including the Table of Contents and the entry words. Ask students to notice which words were selected and how the words are organized in the mini-book.

Point out the blank spaces on each page. Ask students what these lines can be used for. Direct the students' attention to the blank pages at the back of the book. Encourage students to use these pages to add new words they may want to use in their writing.

Lesson Plan Idea

Select a piece of writing that has very limited word choice to share with your students. Copy the story onto an overlay and ask students to offer comments about the story.

Then ask students to use their *Marvelous Thesaurus* to look for more descriptive words. Using a blank overlay, rewrite the story with the words supplied by your students. Take time to compare the two pieces of writing.

My Book of Great Grammar Rules

Introducing the Mini-Book

Begin by asking students to describe important elements in writing such as the use of capital letters, periods, commas, etc. Discuss them with students. Next, give students their assembled mini-books and ask them to read the Table of Contents.

Review each of the pages with students while reinforcing the importance of referring to this guide whenever a question about grammar rules arises.

Lesson Plan Idea

Write a set of sentences on the board that have errors such as missing punctuation. Tell students that each sentence has at least one error, and that they must find the grammar rule in their mini-books that applies to each error.

Allow time for students to look up the information and to discuss each sentence. Ask students to approach the board to make the necessary corrections to each sentence.

My Rhyming Word Dictionary

Introducing the Mini-Book

After giving each student an assembled mini-book, take some time to identify the features of the book including the Table of Contents and the entry words. Ask students to notice which words were selected and how the words are organized in the mini-book.

Lesson Plan Idea

Share a variety of rhyming poems with your students. Then, leave off the rhyming words and ask students to supply the rhyming words by looking up the words in their mini-books.

Encourage students to use their *Rhyming Word Dictionary* whenever they write poetry.

My Wonderful Writing-Prompt Journal

Introducing the Mini-Book

After providing the students with their assembled mini-books, ask students to read the contents and think about possible ways to respond to each prompt.

Lesson Plan Idea

Write a sample story using one of the prompts found in the mini-book and copy onto an overlay.

Begin by telling students that you want them to determine the strengths of this particular piece of writing. As students respond to the story, point out how each mini-book might help improve the story—such as helping with proper spelling, word choice, grammar, and helping with story ideas. Frequently reinforce the importance and helpfulness of each mini-book.

My Super Spelling Dictionary

could

because

about

This book belongs to

_____

Zz

zipper

zoo

zigzag

zillion

about   any

always   away

Dear Students,

You are going to love this personal dictionary! It has one page for every letter of the alphabet.

Turn to this book every time you think of a word that you want to write, but are not quite sure how to spell. If the word isn't already in your dictionary, find the correct spelling and add it to help you in the future.

By the time the school year ends, you'll be surprised at all the new words you've learned.

Happy Spelling & Writing!

Cc

come
could

can't
children

5

Bb

believe
brought

beautiful
because

4

Ee

enough

every

each

either

Dd

different

does

dear

didn't

Gg

grow

guest

goes

great

Ff

friend

from

family

fast

Hh

holiday
how

have
haven't

Ii

interesting
isn't

idea
incredible

Jj

January
joyful

jump
just

12

Kk

kind
knew

know
knowledge

13

Ll

little
loss

laugh
learn

Mm

most
mysterious

many
marvelous

only

outside

often

once

now

number

neighbor

nothing

Pp

party   people

please   pretty

Qq

question   quick

quiet   quite

something

surprise

said

seen

rhyme

right

really

reason

Uu

upon

useful

under

unusual

Tt

they

they're

their

there

Ww

when
which

was
what

25

Vv

vegetable
very

valentine
vanish

24

Yy

you're
you've

yesterday
young

Xx

x-ray

xerox
xylophone

My Marvelous Pocket Thesaurus

jolly

silly

funny

This book belongs to

_____

Words to use instead of _____

(Add your word here.)

1. _____

2. _____

3. _____

4. _____

5. _____

6. _____

7. _____

8. _____

9. _____

10. _____

11. _____

12. _____

13. _____

14. _____

15. _____

16. _____

Dear Student,

Words are powerful. They help us express what we think and feel. But sometimes it's hard to think of exactly the right words to use.

This thesaurus (pronounced the-SOR-us) is here to help! You can use it to find just the word you need so you don't have to use the same words over and over and over and over again. It may even teach you some new words, too.

Happy Writing!

Table of Contents

Words to use instead of

⭐ bad ⭐
(adjective)

1. naughty
2. wicked
3. vile
4. sinister
5. corrupt
6. hurtful
7. harmful
8. evil

9. disobedient
10. mischievous
11. unfavorable
12. displeasing
13. _____
14. _____
15. _____
16. _____

Words to use instead of

⭐ ask ⭐
(verb)

1. inquire
2. query
3. interrogate
4. question
5. request
6. beg
7. beseech
8. implore

9. entreat
10. make an inquiry
11. examine
12. seek information
13. _____
14. _____
15. _____
16. _____

Words to use instead of **big** (adjective)

1. large
2. huge
3. great
4. enormous
5. giant
6. gigantic
7. vast
8. mammoth

9. immense
10. colossal
11. broad
12. vast
13. _____
14. _____
15. _____
16. _____

Words to use instead of **funny** (adjective)

1. hilarious
2. amusing
3. comical
4. humorous
5. silly
6. jolly
7. ridiculous
8. laughable

9. witty
10. rib-tickling
11. absurd
12. whimsical
13. _____
14. _____
15. _____
16. _____

Words to use instead of

happy
(adjective)

1. cheerful

2. glad

3. pleasant

4. upbeat

5. thrilled

6. joyful

7. delighted

8. content

9. merry

10. overjoyed

11. blissful

12. ecstatic

13. _____

14. _____

15. _____

16. _____

Words to use instead of

good
(adjective)

1. great

2. grand

3. wonderful

4. terrific

5. excellent

6. marvelous

7. fabulous

8. fantastic

9. outstanding

10. magnificent

11. stupendous

12. benevolent

13. _____

14. _____

15. _____

16. _____

Words to use instead of

nice
(adjective)

1. lovely
2. delightful
3. pleasant
4. enjoyable
5. wonderful
6. excellent
7. fine
8. kind

9. likable
10. pleasing
11. agreeable
12. proper
13. _____
14. _____
15. _____
16. _____

Words to use instead of

lots
(adjective)

1. many
2. tons
3. plenty
4. extra
5. loads
6. scads
7. millions
8. myriad

9. numerous
10. innumerable
11. copious
12. numberless
13. _____
14. _____
15. _____
16. _____

Words to use instead of **sad** ☆☆
(adjective)

1. unhappy	9. mournful
2. melancholy	10. dismal
3. morose	11. despondent
4. dejected	12. dispirited
5. sorrowful	13. _____
6. downhearted	14. _____
7. gloomy	15. _____
8. somber	16. _____

Words to use instead of ☆ **pretty** ☆☆
(adjective)

1. beautiful	9. graceful
2. lovely	10. stunning
3. gorgeous	11. attractive
4. handsome	12. pleasing
5. glamorous	13. _____
6. cute	14. _____
7. delightful	15. _____
8. good-looking	16. _____

Words to use instead of

small (adjective)

1. little
2. tiny
3. miniature
4. petite
5. diminutive
6. trivial
7. insignificant
8. minor
9. unimportant
10. petty
11. trifling
12. peewee
13. _____
14. _____
15. _____
16. _____

Words to use instead of

said (verb)

1. replied
2. answered
3. muttered
4. mumbled
5. yelled
6. screamed
7. called
8. demanded
9. cheered
10. whispered
11. mouthed
12. uttered
13. _____
14. _____
15. _____
16. _____

Words to use instead of **walk**

(verb)

1. stroll
2. saunter
3. hike
4. march
5. pace
6. tramp
7. promenade
8. traipse
9. trek
10. trudge
11. ramble
12. dash
13. _____
14. _____
15. _____
16. _____

Words to use instead of **smart**

(adjective)

1. bright
2. intelligent
3. brainy
4. clever
5. brilliant
6. keen
7. sharp
8. knowledgeable
9. penetrating
10. resourceful
11. adroit
12. quick
13. _____
14. _____
15. _____
16. _____

Words to use instead of

(Add your word here.)

1. _____
2. _____
3. _____
4. _____
5. _____
6. _____
7. _____
8. _____
9. _____
10. _____
11. _____
12. _____
13. _____
14. _____
15. _____
16. _____

Words to use instead of

(Add your word here.)

1. _____
2. _____
3. _____
4. _____
5. _____
6. _____
7. _____
8. _____
9. _____
10. _____
11. _____
12. _____
13. _____
14. _____
15. _____
16. _____

My Book of Great Grammar Rules

This book belongs to _____

Making Nouns Plural

We use the plural form of a noun to show that there is more than one object.

It's easy to remember how to make nouns plural.

★ **The plurals of most nouns are formed by adding s.**

Example: dog ⇨ dogs, cat ⇨ cats

Write the plural form for table and elephant.

_____

★ **Add s to words ending in a vowel + y.**

Example: boy ⇨ boys, toy ⇨ toys

Write the plural form for play and way.

_____

★ **Add es to words ending in s, x, z, ch, and sh.**

Example: class ⇨ classes, fox ⇨ foxes

Write the plural form for glass and rush.

_____

★ **Change y to i and add es to words ending with a consonant + y.**

Example: cherry ⇨ cherries

Write the plural form for puppy and baby.

_____

Dear Student,

Being able to write well is one of the most important things you'll ever learn. But, while using words to express ideas and feelings is exciting, it can be frustrating, too. English has some tricky grammar rules.

That's why we created this handy mini-guide. It will help you learn and remember these must-know rules. Once you learn them, you'll discover that grammar can be great fun. And, surprise! You'll become a better writer and reader, too!

Happy Learning!

Table of Contents

☆ When to Capitalize a Word ☆

It's easy to remember when to use a capital letter:

★ **Whenever you use the word *I*.**

★ **Whenever you begin a sentence.**

★ **Whenever you write a person's first, middle, or last name.**

Example: George Washington

Try it for yourself. Write your full name here:

_____

★ **Whenever you write a month, a day of the week, or a holiday.**

Example: This year, Thanksgiving is on Thursday, November 20.

Try it for yourself. Write the name and date of your favorite holiday here:

_____

★ **Whenever you write the name of a country, state, or city.**

Example: San Francisco, California

Try it for yourself. Write the name of your city and state here:

_____

☆ Parts of Speech ☆

noun
A word that is used to name any person, place, or thing.

Examples: George Washington, Disneyland, candy

verb
A word that is used to show action.

Examples: run, leap, throw

adjective
A word that is used to describe a noun.

Examples: red, big, old

adverb
A word that is used to tell how, when, or where.

Examples: slowly, quickly, immediately

☆ When to Use a Period ☆

The period's greatest responsibility is to end a sentence. But periods also end commands and requests, and are used to punctuate initials and abbreviations.

It's easy to remember when to use a period.

★ **Use a period to end a sentence.**

Example: Daniel ate a tasty piece of pizza.

Try it for yourself. Write a sentence about your favorite food here:

_____

★ **Use a period to end a command.**

Example: Lucky, stop eating that bone.

Try it for yourself. Write a command for a pet here:

_____

★ **Whenever you write an address.**

Example: 1600 Pennsylvania Avenue

Try it for yourself. Write your address here:

_____

★ **Whenever you write the name of a special place.**

Example: Yellowstone National Park

Try it for yourself. Write the name of your favorite place here:

_____

★ **Whenever you write the title of a story, book, movie, song, or poem.**

Example: The Wizard of Oz

Try it for yourself. Write the name of your favorite books here:

_____

It's easy to remember when to use a comma.

★ **Use a comma to separate three or more items in a series.**

Example: I have a dog, a cat, and a pet iguana.

Try it for yourself. Write a sentence about three animals that you might see in the zoo.

_____

★ **Use a comma to separate phrases that are joined with conjunctions—words such as *and, but, for, yet,* or *so.***

Example: I like pizza, but spaghetti is really my favorite food.

Try it for yourself. Write a sentence about your favorite food using a comma and the words and, but, for, yet, or so.

_____

★ **Use a comma before using quotation marks.**

Example: The bear said, "I have to find more honey."

Try it for yourself. Write a sentence that tells what the bear says after he finds a tree full of honey.

_____

★ **Use a period for a request.**

Example: Mom, please give me a glass of milk.

Try it for yourself. Write a request for an ice cream cone:

_____

★ **Use a period to punctuate initials.**

Example: • W.C. Fields

• George W. Bush

• He attended college at U.C.L.A.

Try it for yourself. Use initials to write the names of some of your friends here:

_____

_____

☆

☆ When to Use Quotation Marks ☆

It's easy to remember when to use quotation marks.

★ **Use quotation marks for a direct quotation.**

Example: Helen Keller once said, "Keep your face toward the sunshine and you won't see the shadow."

Try it for yourself. Find a quotation from a famous person in history. Write the quote in the space below using quotation marks.

_____

_____

★ **Use quotation marks to show dialogue in your writing.**

Example: "Put that dog on a leash!" cried the angry dog catcher.

Try it for yourself. Write a sentence that uses dialogue.

_____

_____

★ **Use a comma when writing the date.**

Example: The Declaration of Independence was signed on July 4, 1776.

Try it for yourself. Write a sentence that tells when you were born.

_____

★ **Use a comma between the name of a city and the state, district, or country.**

Example: • She lives in Seattle, Washington.

• He lives in Madison, Wisconsin.

Try it for yourself. Write a sentence about where you live. Include the city and state.

_____

Try it for yourself again. Write a sentence about where you might want to live when you grow up.

_____

☆ **Contractions** ☆

A contraction is a short form of two words. An apostrophe is used in place of the missing letter or letters.

Examples:

are not = aren't	must not = mustn't
can not = can't	she will = she'll
could not = couldn't	should not = shouldn't
has not = hasn't	they are = they're
have not = haven't	they will = they'll
here is = here's	we are = we're
I am = I'm	we will = we'll
I did = I'd	will not = won't
I have = I've	would not = wouldn't
it is = it's	you are = you're
is not = isn't	I will = I'll
I would = I'd	let us = let's

★ **Use quotation marks to show the name of a poem, song, movie, story, or chapter in a book.**

Example:
- Did you read the poem, "When Tillie Ate the Chili" by Jack Prelutsky?
- My favorite song is "Yesterday."
- Have you seen the new "Star Wars" movie?
- The teacher read "Little Red Riding Hood" to her class.

Try it for yourself. Write a sentence that tells about your favorite movie.

_____

_____

Try it for yourself again. Write a sentence about your favorite song.

_____

_____

_____

☆ Using To, Too, and Two ☆

It's easy to remember when to use to, too, and two.

To
★ Use *to* to tell direction.

Example: He will turn to the right.

Try it for yourself. Write a sentence using the word to.

_____

_____

Too
★ Use *too* to show more than, or in place of the word *also.*

Example: • She ate too many cookies.
• She had a tummy ache, too.

Try it for yourself. Write a sentence that uses the word too.

_____

_____

Two
★ Use *two* to show the number 2.

Example: She is two years old.

Try it for yourself. Write a sentence using the number word two.

_____

_____

☆ Using There, Their, and They're ☆

It's easy to remember when to use there, their, and they're.

There
★ Use *there* to tell about a place.

Example: His house is over there.

Try it for yourself. Write a sentence using the word there.

_____

_____

Their
★ Use *their* to tell about belonging.

Example: Their house is big.

Try it for yourself. Write a sentence using the word their.

_____

_____

They're
★ Use the contraction, *they're,* for the words *they are.*

Example: They're reading the new mystery book.

Try it for yourself. Write a sentence that tells what your friends are doing using the word they're.

_____

_____

My Rhyming Dictionary

pace

face

ace

This book belongs to

_____

— Y —

Look Alike, Sound Alike Rhymes

apply	fry	sly
butterfly	my	spry
by	nearby	spy
classify	pry	try
cry	rely	why
deny	satisfy	wry
dry	shy	
fly	sky	

Sound Alike Rhymes

buy	hi	sigh
bye	high	thigh
eye	I	tie
good-bye	lie	untie
guy	pie	

My Ideas

_____ y   _____ y

_____ y   _____ y

_____ ace

Look Alike, Sound Alike Rhymes

ace	pace	space
face	place	trace
lace	replace	
misplace	shoelace	

Sound Alike Rhymes

base	chase	vase
bass	erase	
case	suitcase	

My Ideas

_____ ace   _____ ace

_____ ace   _____ ace

Dear Students,

This book is really easy to use! All you need to do is turn to the page with the rhyming sound you are looking for. Rhyming sounds begin with a vowel (a, e, i, o, u, and sometimes y).

There are *three* sections on each page.

★ The first section lists *perfect* rhymes. These are rhymes that both look and sound alike.

★ The second section lists *imperfect* rhymes. These are words that sound alike, but do not contain the same letter pattern.

★ The third section is for you! It's a place where you can add any new rhyming words you find through your reading and schoolwork.

Happy Rhyming!

air

Look Alike, Sound Alike Rhymes

air	hair	stair
chair	lair	unfair
fair	pair	
flair	repair	

Sound Alike Rhymes

bare	hare	stare
bear	mare	tear
care	pear	their
dare	rare	there
fare	scare	wear
flare	share	where
glare	square	

My Ideas

_____ air

_____ air

_____ air

_____ air

ake

Look Alike, Sound Alike Rhymes

bake	lake	shake
brake	make	snake
cake	quake	stake
fake	rake	take
flake	sake	wake

Sound Alike Rhymes

ache	break	toothache
bellyache	steak	

My Ideas

_____ ake

_____ ake

_____ ake

_____ ake

___ at

Look Alike, Sound Alike Rhymes

acrobat	democrat	mat
at	fat	pat
bat	flat	rat
brat	format	sat
cat	habitat	that
chat	hat	wildcat

My Ideas

_____ at

_____ at

_____ at

_____ at

___ an

Look Alike, Sound Alike Rhymes

an	Japan	Superman
ban	man	tan
Batman	pan	than
began	plan	van
caravan	ran	
fan	scan	

My Ideas

_____ an

_____ an

_____ an

_____ an

Look Alike, Sound Alike Rhymes

agree	flee	see
bee	free	teepee
degree	glee	three
fee	knee	tree

Sound Alike Rhymes

be	me	she
flea	monkey	ski
he	pea	tea
key	sea	we

My Ideas

ee _____   ee _____

ee _____   ee _____

Look Alike, Sound Alike Rhymes

bed	fled	sled
bled	led	shred
bred	red	sped
fed	shed	wed

Sound Alike Rhymes

ahead	head	said
bread	instead	spread
dead	lead	thread
dread	read	

My Ideas

ed _____   ed _____

ed _____   ed _____

_____ en

Look Alike, Sound Alike Rhymes

den	pen	when
hen	ten	yen
men	then	

Sound Alike Rhymes

again	been

My Ideas

_____ en

_____ en

_____ en

_____ en

_____ eed

Look Alike, Sound Alike Rhymes

agreed	feed	proceed
breed	freed	reed
creed	greed	seed
deed	heed	speed
disagreed	indeed	succeed
exceed	need	weed

Sound Alike Rhymes

bead	plead	stampede
lead	read	supercede
mislead	skied	

My Ideas

_____ eed

_____ eed

_____ eed

_____ eed

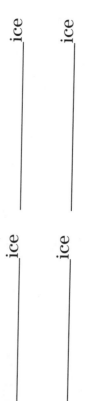

_____ ice

Look Alike, Sound Alike Rhymes

advice	mice
dice	nice
ice	price
lice	rice
slice	
spice	
twice	

Sound Alike Rhymes

paradise	precise

My Ideas

_____ ice

_____ ice

_____ ice

_____ ice

_____ ent

Look Alike, Sound Alike Rhymes

bent	sent
cent	spent
content	tent
dent	vent
event	went
gent	
invent	
present	
rent	
scent	

Sound Alike Rhymes

meant

My Ideas

_____ ent

_____ ent

_____ ent

_____ ent

★ ___ ike ★

Look Alike, Sound Alike Rhymes

alike	hike	spike
bike	like	unlike
dislike	motorbike	
childlike	pike	

Sound Alike Rhymes

tyke

My Ideas

_____ ike   _____ ike

_____ ike   _____ ike

★ ___ ide ★

Look Alike, Sound Alike Rhymes

bride	hide	side
decide	inside	slide
divide	outside	snide
glide	pride	tide
guide	ride	wide

Sound Alike Rhymes

applied	multiplied	sighed
cried	occupied	spied
dried	pried	tied
fried	replied	tried
lied	satisfied	untied
magnified	shied	

My Ideas

_____ ide   _____ ide

_____ ide   _____ ide

in

Look Alike, Sound Alike Rhymes

begin	spin
bin	thin
chin	tin
din	twin
fin	win
grin	within

Sound Alike Rhymes

again	captain
been	inn

My Ideas

_____ in

_____ in

_____ in

_____ in

---

ing

Look Alike, Sound Alike Rhymes

anything	king	something
bring	ring	thing
cling	sing	wing
ding	spring	zing
everything	sting	
fling	string	

My Ideas

_____ ing

_____ ing

_____ ing

_____ ing

____ ock ☆

Look Alike, Sound Alike Rhymes

block	jock	rock
clock	knock	shock
dock	lock	sock
flock	mock	stock

Sound Alike Rhymes

chalk	hawk	talk
gawk	squawk	walk

My Ideas

_____ ock _____ ock

_____ ock _____ ock

____ it ☆

Look Alike, Sound Alike Rhymes

admit	kit	pit
bit	knit	quit
fit	lit	sit
flit	misfit	skit
grit	moonlit	slit
hit	omit	spit
it	permit	wit

Sound Alike Rhymes

counterfeit	get	mitt
forget	helmet	separate

My Ideas

_____ it _____ it

_____ it _____ it

Look Alike, Sound Alike Rhymes

awoke	joke	stroke
broke	poke	woke
choke	smoke	

Sound Alike Rhymes

croak	oak	yolk
folk	soak	

My Ideas

_____oke   _____oke

_____oke   _____oke

Look Alike, Sound Alike Rhymes

behold	gold	scold
blindfold	hold	sold
bold	mold	told
cold	old	
fold	retold	

Sound Alike Rhymes

bowled	rolled	strolled
polled		

My Ideas

_____old   _____old

_____old   _____old

_____ out

Look Alike, Sound Alike Rhymes

about	scout	stout
bout	shout	throughout
clout	snout	trout
out	spout	without
pout	sprout	workout

Sound Alike Rhymes

| doubt | drought | route |

My Ideas

_____ out

_____ out

_____ out

_____ out

_____ op

Look Alike, Sound Alike Rhymes

bop	mountaintop	stop
chop	plop	teardrop
crop	pop	tiptop
drop	prop	top
flop	raindrop	treetop
hop	shortstop	workshop
mop	shop	

Sound Alike Rhymes

swap

My Ideas

_____ op

_____ op

_____ op

_____ op

ump

Look Alike, Sound Alike Rhymes

bump	jump	stump
chump	lump	thump
dump	plump	
grump	rump	
hump	slump	

My Ideas

_____ ump

_____ ump

_____ ump

_____ ump

---

um

Look Alike, Sound Alike Rhymes

bum	gum	sum
chum	hum	yum
drum	plum	
glum	mum	

Sound Alike Rhymes

become	dumb	overcome
come	from	some
crumb	numb	thumb

My Ideas

_____ um

_____ um

_____ um

_____ um

_____ ut

Look Alike, Sound Alike Rhymes

but	haircut	shortcut
coconut	hut	shut
cut	jut	strut
glut	nut	
gut	rut	

My Ideas

_____ ut

_____ ut

_____ ut

_____ ut

_____ unch

Look Alike, Sound Alike Rhymes

brunch	hunch	punch
bunch	lunch	scrunch
crunch	munch	

My Ideas

_____ unch

_____ unch

_____ unch

_____ unch

My Wonderful ☆
Writing-Prompt ☆
Journal

feelings

dreams

hopes

This book belongs to

_____

My Someday Wishes and Dreams ☆

When Amelia Earhart was a little girl, she dreamed of flying. When she grew up, she became the world's most famous woman pilot. Write about your wishes and what might happen if they come true.

_____

_____

_____

_____

_____

_____

_____

_____

☆

Write Your Own Food Riddle

Write four clues about your favorite food. Be sure your clues are full of great descriptions, but do *not* reveal the name of your favorite food.

Share your clues with a friend. See if he or she can guess the answer.

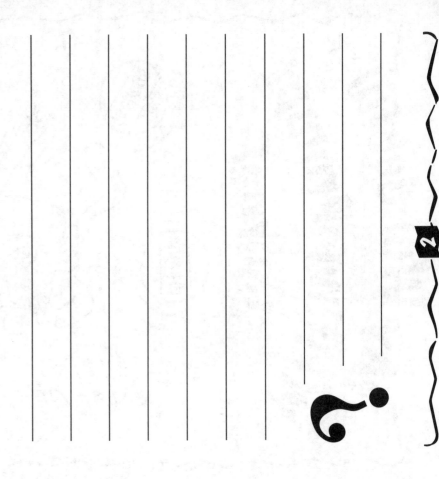

_____

_____

_____

_____

_____

_____

_____

_____

_____

Dear Student,

Writing can be great fun. It's a way for you to express your hopes, dreams, feelings, and imagination. But sometimes it can be hard to come up with great ideas to write about.

That's where this book comes in. It's chock-full of all kinds of super prompts to make writing fun and meaningful. Now grab a pencil and get creative!

Happy Imagineering!

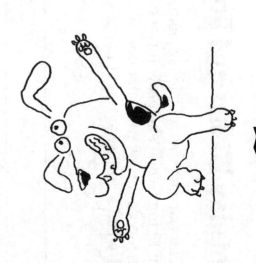

Sign of the Times (continued)

_____

_____

_____

_____

_____

_____

_____

_____

_____

_____

_____

_____

Sign of the Times

In the box below, design a sign that shows something that is really important to you.

Then describe in words what the sign says about you.

_____

_____

_____

_____

_____

Animal Crackers (continued)

☆

_____

_____

_____

_____

_____

_____

_____

_____

_____

_____

_____

_____

6

Animal Crackers

☆

What a weird box of animal crackers! When I
opened it up, you'll never guess what happened...

_____

_____

_____

_____

_____

_____

_____

_____

_____

_____

_____

5

Guess Who Followed Me Home? *(continued)*

☆

☆

8

Guess Who Followed Me Home?

As I headed home from school today, I noticed a very cute _____ was following me, so I...

(animal)

☆

7

Imagine That! My New Invention (continued)

Imagine That! My New Invention

Thomas Edison created over 1,093 inventions, including the electric light bulb and the phonograph.

Pretend you are a famous inventor. Describe one of your inventions and how it will help make the world a better place.

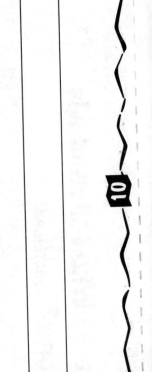

Trading Places (continued)

☆

_____

_____

_____

_____

_____

_____

_____

_____

_____

_____

_____

_____

_____

_____

12

Trading Places

☆ ☆

If you could change places with anyone in the world, who would it be? Use your imagination and describe what your life would be like.

_____

_____

_____

_____

_____

_____

_____

_____

_____

_____

_____

_____

_____

☆

11

The Magic Key (continued)

☆

☆

The Magic Key

☆

The man in the magic shop handed me an old, gold key. "This is a magic key," he whispered. "It will work in any lock!" As soon as I got home, I took the key from my pocket and...

Wacky Wednesday (continued)

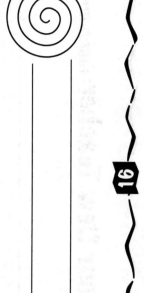

16

Wacky Wednesday

Last Wednesday, I came down to breakfast and I found a chimpanzee flipping pancakes and a brown bear reading the newspaper. The next thing I saw was...

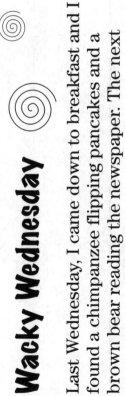

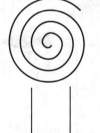

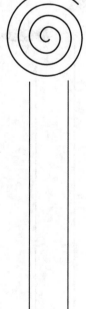

15

Meet Your New Teacher *(continued)*

Meet Your New Teacher

One day our principal opened the door to our classroom. In a cheery voice she said, "Let me introduce you to your new teacher, Alvin Anteater." Mr. Anteater walked in and…

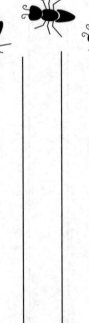

School Rules (continued)

☆

School Rules

☆   ☆

You have been given the chance to change your school's rules. Explain what rules you would change and why.

My Hero (continued)

_____
_____
_____
_____
_____
_____
_____
_____
_____
_____
_____
_____
_____
_____
_____

My Hero ☆

Write about your hero. What makes this person someone whom you admire and look up to? Draw a picture of your hero in the box below. Then write about him or her.

_____
_____
_____
_____
_____
_____
_____
_____

The Best Time (continued)

(lined writing space)

24

The Best Time

What was the very best time you ever had? Where did you go? What did you do? Write all about this special time and don't leave out a single detail!

(lined writing space)

23

The Peculiar Pet Store (continued)

The Peculiar Pet Store

There's a new pet store in town that's very peculiar. It doesn't sell guinea pigs, parrots, or fish like most pet stores. It sells…

In the box below, draw a picture of the animals this pet store sells. Then describe each animal in detail.

Teacher's Notes

Teacher's Notes

Teacher's Notes

Teacher's Notes